Change the World for a Fiver

KT-430-687

Change the World for a Fiver has been published to mark the launch of We Are What We Do, a project of Community Links.

First published in Great Britain in 2004 by Short Books Ltd, 15 Highbury Terrace, London N5 1UP.

Copyright © Community Links Trust Ltd.

The moral right of the authors has been asserted.

ISBN 1 904095 96 8

A CIP catalogue record for this book is available from the British Library.

All rights reserved. No part of this book may be reproduced in any form or by any means without permission in writing from the publisher, except by a reviewer who may quote passages and reproduce images for the purposes of a review.

Printed in United Kingdom by St Ives Westerham Press.

Printed on chlorine-free paper from trees grown in sustainable forests.

Change the World for a Fiver

50 actions to change the world and make you feel good

Designed by Antidote
Creative team: Tim Ashton, Steve Henry, Ken Hoggins, Chris O'Shea,
Chris Wigan, David Robinson, Eugénie Harvey and Paul Twivy.

The development of We Are What We Do is led by Eugénie Harvey.
The project has been generously supported by the Joffe Charitable Trust.

 SHORT BOOKS

we are what we do ©

We Are What We Do is a Community Links project
(registered charity number 1018517). Community
Links tackles the causes and consequences of
social exclusion in east London and shares the
local experience with practitioners and policy
makers nationwide.

We believe in acting local and thinking global.

Everyone who has contributed to the book has done
so for free. Money raised from the sales of the book
will be used to cover the costs of production. This
means that the book is worth double, triple, possibly
even quadruple the money you've paid for it.

Should we re-print the book, money raised from sales
will be used by Community Links to fund other We Are
What We Do projects.

For further information about We Are What We Do,
or to make comments or suggestions, please visit
www.wearewhatwedo.org

For further information about Community Links,
please visit www.community-links.org

community links

We live in peculiar times. More communications devices than ever before can connect us, yet more people live alone. We want to belong to communities but our cities can be very lonely places.

We buy things – more and more things – with more and more money; but they don't make us happy – life satisfaction was higher during post-war rationing in the 1940s.

The rich are getting richer, but 1 in 5 Britons are still shockingly poor. The other 4 out of 5 experience other kinds of poverty: most of us feel that our lives are missing something.

Voting in elections is declining and membership of political parties has fallen by two thirds over a single generation. Yet the UK has recently witnessed its biggest ever street demonstrations designed to change government policies on issues as diverse as world debt, fox hunting and the war against Iraq.

We feel things very deeply and we want to do something, but what?

It was Mahatma Gandhi who said: 'We must be the change we want to see in the world'. In other words, we are what we do.

So why is it so difficult?

Perhaps it is the scale of the problems which induces the state of paralysis. We think we have to leave change to governments or big business even though we also know that we elect governments and that our spending is what creates big business.

Surely the question now is not whether we should act alone but how can we act together.

We Are What We Do is not a charity. It is not an institution. It is a new kind of movement – a movement with attitude. We are not trying to raise money. We are trying to show the power of a simple shift in attitudes and day-to-day behaviour.

We invite you to be part of a new kind of community; not of joiners but of independent doers following the same banner and answering the questions that we all want answered.

Who are we? We Are What We Do.

How to use this book

This is a book of simple, everyday actions which we reckon pretty much all of us can do. If you're reading this book, chances are you, or someone you know, has actually done one of the actions already (Action 33 Recycle Your Books or Action 47 Buy a Copy of This Book for a Friend) so you're already on the way!

Each page has an action strip down the right-hand side. This says what the action is.

A number of pages feature references to organisations which can help you perform the actions – for example, Action 26 Give Blood features the website addresses for all the blood donor organisations in England, Scotland, Ireland and Wales.

We've included a whole host of related websites in Action 49 Learn More, Do More, at the end of the book which will give you more information about the action and how to do it.

We're not suggesting that either the list of actions or of websites in Action 49 are definitive – but they are a start. We'd love to hear from you, either with suggestions for new actions, or suggestions for other helpful organisations and websites. Please email us at suggestions@wearewhatwedo.org and check out our website to see updated lists of both.

The 500 year shopping trip

Every person in the country uses an average of 134 plastic bags every year.

That's 8 billion bags all together.

A plastic bag can take up to 500 years to decay in landfill.

There is an alternative.

It's called a shopping bag, and apparently in France, it's very chic.

Photo: Struan Wallace

Illustration: Sholto Walker at illustrationweb.com

When kids ask you to read a story to them, it's because they know something you don't.
They know you'll both feel richer for the experience.

Capture a child's imagination...

Photo: Kevin Anthony Horgan / Getty Images

Change a light bulb and see what you can save

An energy saving light bulb might not seem cheap but over its lifetime it could save you 65 quid and a lot more besides. Like the planet for example.

Learning first aid is child's play.

It only takes two hours to learn how to save a life.

What else are you going to do in that time that is going to make such a difference?

Watch 'Stars in their Eyes' twice over?

And let's face it, saving someone's life is cool. In fact, it's about as cool as you can possibly get.

And, if you do learn this skill, you might like to know that the person you help is statistically unlikely to be a stranger.

They're more likely to be a friend or relative.

Imagine saving your best friend's life.

Photo: Judy Lambert / Getty Images

It takes half as many
muscles to smile as
it does to frown.

And it makes you
and others feel twice
as good.

Illustration: Andrew Selby at illustrationweb.com

A double-decker bus carries the same number of people as 40 cars. And it's going there anyway.

5 Scots Pine
seeds

Illustration: Ruth Palmer at illustrationweb.com

5 Scots Pine seeds

Illustration: Ruth Palmer at illustrationweb.com

A double-decker bus carries the same number of people as 40 cars. And it's going there anyway.

Your very own 2012 Christmas Tree

Trees are amazing things. They take in stuff we don't like (carbon dioxide) and pump out stuff we do (oxygen). But we get rid of these amazing things by the million every year. In fact, 33 soccer pitches of trees are cut down every minute worldwide.

However, you can do something to help. And you don't need to be able to tell your Dimmocks from your Titchmarsh to do it.

Just follow the instructions on the packet opposite.

And, once you've done it, you can gather the family round on Christmas morning, point to your masterpiece and say – 'That's it. That's my Christmas present to all of you, for the next 100 years.'

Each tree will provide oxygen for two people for the rest of their lives.

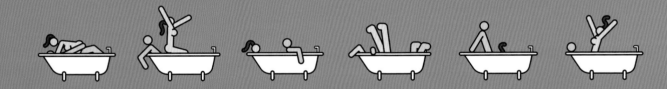

Save water. Have fun. Just get out before everything becomes wrinkled.

Illustration: Andy Holmes at Three Blind Mice

$$35 = 30 \times 2$$

Photo: Spencer Jones / Shannon Fagan / Getty Images

At 35mph, you are twice as likely to kill someone you hit as at 30mph.

Spot the difference

If you turn your thermostat down by
one degree, you can save on average
£25 a year.

That's £2 a month you can put
in charity tins (see Action 16).

Photo: John Lamb / Getty Images

Illustration: Willie Ryan at illustrationweb.com

Walk more

Obesity is turning into a massive problem in the developed world.

One suggestion from doctors is to do something simple such as walking up a couple of flights of stairs every day.

Although, if you are obese, you're not going to want to do this because inevitably you'll sweat a lot. Which will draw attention to the very thing you're trying to deal with.

So much for doctors.

But try walking as much as you can.

If that's only from the dessert trolley to the cheese board and back again – well, that's a starter.

Well, no it isn't – it's a pudding. But you get the idea.

Photo: Bryan Mullennix / Getty Images

A TV that's on standby is still using a lot of electricity

And a video recorder on standby uses almost as much electricity as one playing a tape.

Switching that little 'standby' light from green to red doesn't actually do you, or the planet, much good.

It's still costing you money and wasting energy.

Illustration: Tim Ashton / Antidote

Don't forget to fone bak

There are 15 million mobile phones replaced in the UK every year.

That's a hell of a lot of annoying ringtones, and worse, it equates to 1500 tonnes of landfill. That's about the same as burying a World War 2 destroyer.

And despite the strong desire to grab the bloke on the train's Flip Up 2200 and chuck it in the nearest bin, resist.

The least irritating thing about your mobile should be what use it can be put to after its death.

Go to www.fonebak.org or drop it in to a mobile phone retailer.

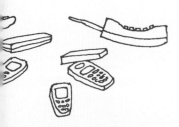

TALK TO OLD PEOPLE

THEY KNOW COOL STUFF YOU DON'T

Photo: Tim Ashton / Antidote

TALK TO YOUNG PEOPLE THEY KNOW COOL STUFF YOU DON'T

REGISTER AS A DONOR ONLINE

After you've died, let your heart beat inside someone else's chest.

Let your liver live, after you've passed on.

Even your eyes could give someone else a new look.

90% of us support organ donation in principle, but only 18% have joined the organ donation register.

To make sure your wishes are carried out, you need to do two things:

Firstly, tell your next of kin about your wishes. Otherwise, in the heat of their distress, they might easily rescind your decision.

Secondly, register online at www.uktransplant.org.uk

So, next time you're surfing the web – make sure you 'save' before you log off.

Photo: John Lamb / Getty Images

£ 2.97

 £ .96P

 £ 4-99

£ 0.99

 £ .95P

£ 4.99

£ 3.98

£ 2.99

Lose money instantly

There's always loose change – and there are always charity tins.

It's a match made in heaven – like ham and eggs, Morecambe and Wise, or Posh and…, well Posh and 'Hello' magazine.

If we all put our loose change into charity tins, the world would be a lot better off.

So, the next time you buy something priced between 95p and 99p, look around for a charity tin.

After all, 1p per person, per week adds up to £30 million per year.

One word of warning, though. If the golden retriever sitting outside the shop doesn't have a slot in his head, don't try putting your coins in. He won't appreciate it.

Photo: Getty Images

Rearrange your pictures.

Make a cocktail.

File.

Write a song.

Apply make up.

Swim in a pond.

Wear gold.

Revert to childhood.

Stay up all night.

Change your hair colour.

Turn left instead of right.

Streak.

Massage someone.

Dust.

Shave something off.

	Arabic	Chinese	Polish	Bengali
Hello	Salaamu Alaikum (Peace Be Upon You)	Nee How	Czesc	Assalam mu alaikum
Goodbye	Salaamu Alaikum (Peace Be Upon You)	Jie Jian	Do widzenia	Khuda hafeez
Please	Min Fadluk	Ching	Prosze	Doya kore
Thank you	Shukran	Se Se	Dziekuje	Doyno baad
Can I help?	Ma yumkin an as 'ad?	Wo leng bung joma?	Czy moge pomoc?	Shajoy korte pari?
Would you like a cup of tea?	Sawfa anta/anti minal fanjan shai?	Ni yow bu yow yi bay cha?	Czy napijesz sie herbaty?	Aponi ki cha pan korben?

Tamil

Vanakam

Santhipoum

Thayavu

Nintri

Uthavi saiyava?

Unkalku thenri thartuma?

Ma yumkin an as 'ad?

Yes, you can help actually.

Just by learning a few words in a foreign language, it's amazing how much genuine warmth you can generate.

It's not something we Brits tend to do well, but it's a lot easier than you think.

For instance, in Arabic the word for 'hello' is the same as the word for 'goodbye'.

Which is a lovely sentiment, although it could make telephone calls rather confusing.

'...So the dog said...'

Illustration: Gray Jolliffe at illustrationweb.com

Make people laugh at you

Learn at least one good joke.

Laughing tones your stomach, lowers your blood pressure, and makes you healthier. It's scientifically proven.

Even the concentration of salivary immunoglobulin A is raised by laughing - and this guards our respiratory tract from infectious organisms.

But that in itself isn't very funny.

Unlike the story about the bloke who goes into a department store and asks a sales assistant "Do you have a complaints department here?" "No we don't", replies the other, "you fat ugly git."

Make sure your pension fund has the same values as you

Unless you check that your pension is ethically invested, chances are you're supporting the arms industry and companies with poor human and environmental records.

Now, this is a complicated area, and even if you're just thinking about your pension, you deserve some kind of medal.

So, to make this as simple as possible – just ask your pension provider one question: 'Can you ensure that my investments don't harm the planet or hurt my fellow man?'

If we all did that, pension providers would soon take notice.

But don't get caught up in a longer conversation, unless you're desperate for company.

As Woody Allen once said, anybody who wants to know the definition of eternity should try spending an evening talking to a life insurance salesman.

Photo: Stephen Chernin / Getty Images

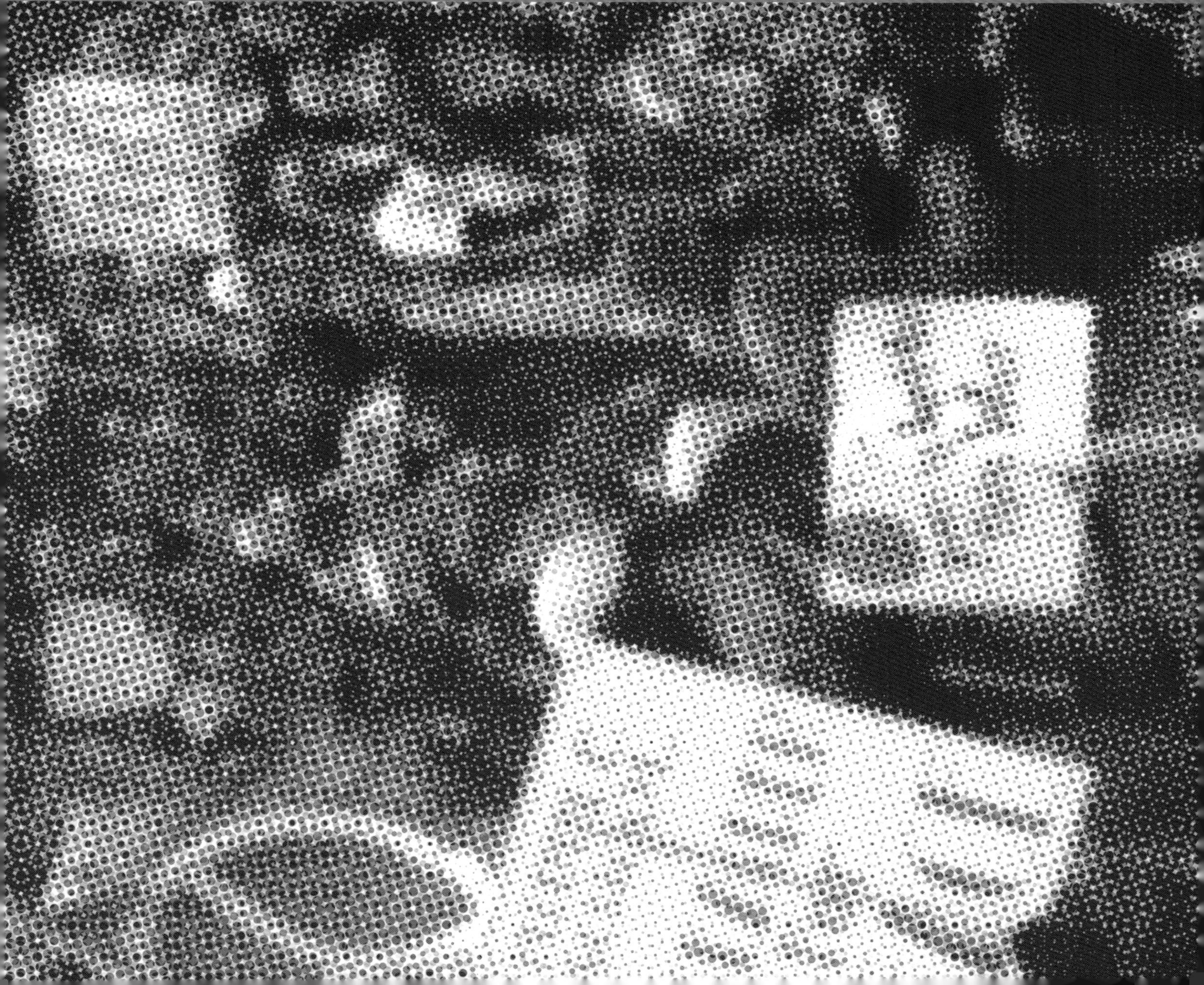

The most beautiful view of Manhattan

Photo: Getty Images

All those offices with lights
burning bright at night.

Are they really all full of
people working late?

Or is it some cock-eyed theory of
aesthetics which says that lighting
an empty space is beautiful?

Ivory was considered beautiful once.

Fur was considered beautiful once.

Samuel Bratt, whose wife would not let him smoke, left her, in 1960, the sum of £330,000 on condition that she smoked five cigars a day.

Amateur footballer Sid Trickett's will in 1982 stipulated that his ashes be scattered at the Torrington Football Club goalmouth where he headed eight goals in 1948.

Dentist Philip Grundy, in 1974, left dental nurse Amelia White £181,000 on condition that she didn't go out with men or wear make-up or jewellery for five years.

In 1990 a lady left £100,000 to the King George Hospital for the 'expansion, improvement and maintenance of its lavatories'.

Ernest Digweed, in 1977, left £26,000 to Jesus provided it could be proved that his identity could be established.

Juan Potomachi, in 1955, left £30,000 to the Teatro Dramatico Theatre provided his skull could be used in Hamlet.

David Davis, in 1788, left his wife five shillings to 'enable her to get drunk for the last time at my expense'.

Hensley Nankivell requested, in 1987, that any relative wanting to benefit from his estate of £400,000 must first train as an airline pilot.

In 1926, Charles Vance Millar, a wealthy Toronto lawyer, bequeathed his estate to whichever woman gave birth to the most babies in the ten-year period following his death.

Have the will to make a will

You can go to a stationer and buy a Make A Will pack for just 99p.

Or you can draw up a will on-line (Action 49).

For helpful advice on making a will, visit www.inlandrevenue.org.uk

And then you can make sure that your goodies don't go to the baddies.

Photo: John Lamb / Getty Images

THE PLEASURE OF THE
COMPANY OF

Our family

IS REQUESTED TONIGHT
AT THE KITCHEN TABLE

TO

GET TOGETHER FOR
A FAMILY MEAL

BRING
CONVERSATION

Research has shown that children who have meals with their parents are much less likely to suffer from anxiety or stress disorders.

So why not try chatting to each other?

George Bush Snr said that America needed more families like the Waltons, and less like the Simpsons.

A very bad idea, as it happens – after all, when was the last time you laughed at the Waltons?

But if you notice, even the Simpsons like to eat together.

Photo: John Lamb / Getty Images

Every year, vending machines in the UK dispense
3 billion polystyrene cups.

Another 3 billion originate from other sources.

Where? Where do they all come from? Is there some
mad genius breeding them in underground bunkers?

Do they sneak out at night and eat our leftovers?

I could have sworn I just saw two of them
whispering to each other.

But why not put your coffee into a mug, not a
plastic cup? It'll taste better, and you'll be doing
your bit for the planet.

It's such a no-brainer – let's make it like wearing fur.

Photo: Chalkie Davis / Getty Images

www.blood.co.uk

www.scotblood.co.uk

www.nibts.org

www.welsh-blood.org.uk

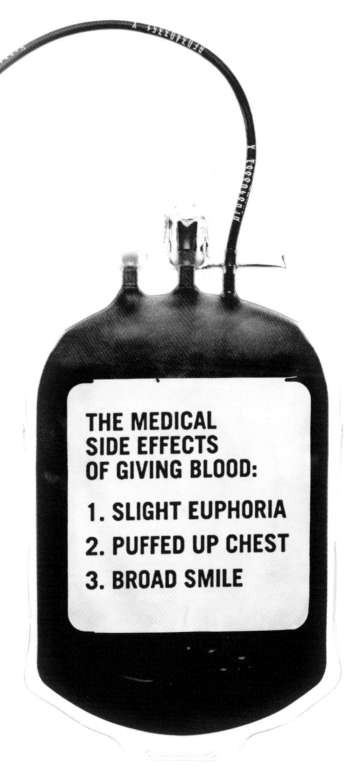

THE MEDICAL
SIDE EFFECTS
OF GIVING BLOOD:

1. SLIGHT EUPHORIA

2. PUFFED UP CHEST

3. BROAD SMILE

Illustration: Paul Daviz at Three Blind Mice

The art of reverse haggling

Confuse the wonderful people who work in charity shops.
Pay them more than they bargained for.

"Be the change you want to see in the world."

Mahatma Gandhi

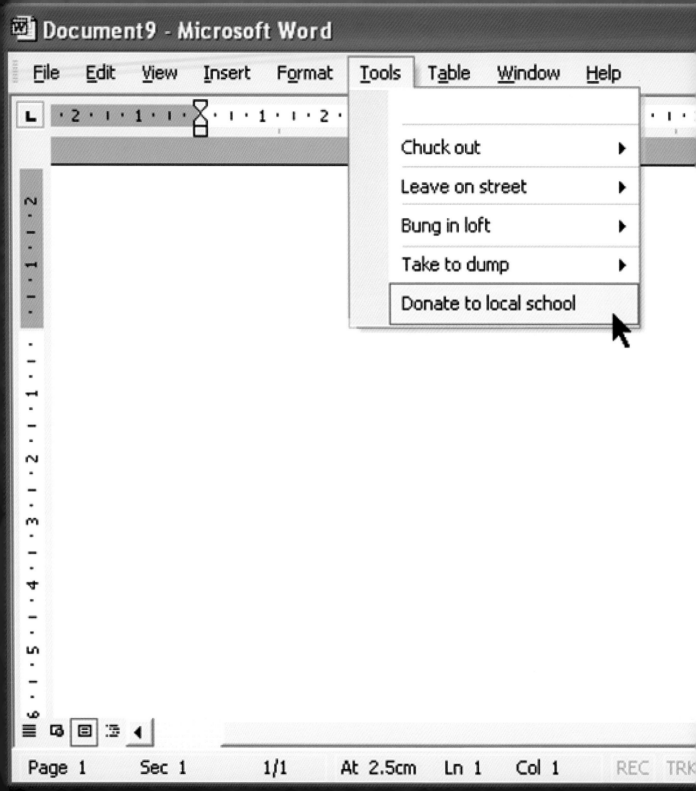

Type a question for help

· 9 · I · 10 · I · 11 · I · 12 · I · 13 · I · 14 · I · 15 · I · 16 · I · 17 · I ·

What we say about glasses in Action 42 applies equally to computers.
Except that computers are slightly heavier to carry down the high street.

So, if you've got a computer you don't need anymore, contact any of the
websites mentioned in Action 49, and they'll help you get it to someone
who can make good use of it here or abroad.

Imagine the joy a seven-year-old in the developing world would feel
if he could play with the mightiest thing ever invented.

The thing you currently use to play 'Minesweeper' and visit dating sites.

OVR   English (U.K

Photo: Nick Walker

Ready, steady, give

Next time you need to buy
a friend a present, don't.
Make them one instead.

Gingerbread Men

110g of softened butter
110g of sugar
1 egg, lightly beaten
2 tablespoon of golden syrup
220g of pain flour
2 teaspoon of baking soda
$\frac{1}{4}$ teaspoon of salt
1 teaspoon of cinnamon
1 teaspoon of ground ginger

Heat oven to 180°C.
Cream butter and sugar.
Beat in the egg and syrup.
Sift in the dry ingredients and mix.
Chill the dough before rolling onto a lightly
floured board, to an $\frac{1}{8}$ inch thickness.
Cut into shapes, using a gingerbread cutter.
Bake on a lightly greased tray for 8–10 minutes.

Give away immediately.

Illustration: Stuart Holmes at illustrationweb.com

Save the world while brushing your teeth

Most people leave the tap running whilst brushing their teeth.

This wastes up to 9 litres of water a minute or 26,000 litres of water per family, per year.

This means your street alone could fill an Olympic sized swimming pool each year.

Which wastes huge amounts of water and is a bit stupid – it's like having the toilet flush the whole time you're on it.

So why not turn off the tap while you clean your teeth?

(We bet this is one of the actions you don't forget from this book. For some reason, it seems to strike a chord with everyone.)

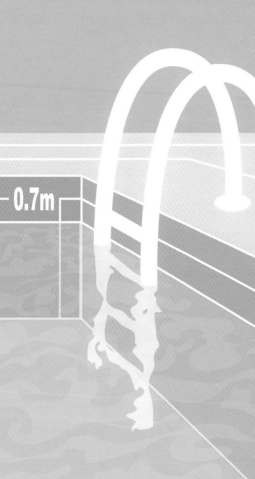

0.7m

Illustration: Chris Wigan / Antidote

Who says you can't draw?

Ever wondered why Rolf Harris looks so cheerful when he's constantly surrounded by dying animals?

Nobody really knows.

But maybe it's because he knows the therapeutic effects of art.

It's fun to draw – and surprisingly easy.

Get a pencil and paper and copy the picture opposite as it is (upside down). Then turn your picture the right way round and, chances are, you've drawn a much better picture than you've ever drawn before.

And you'll find that you've confronted and defeated a prejudice you had about yourself.

Then, if you're inspired, go to our website and pick up more tips on how to do things you've never done before.

J.D. SALINGER

The Catcher in the Rye

Photo: John Lamb / Getty Images

Give away some great ideas

They dreamt up a scheme in Amsterdam a few years ago, whereby white bicycles were provided free. And the idea was that – after you'd finished your ride – you'd leave the bike in the street for someone else to use free.

And if that isn't recycling, we don't know what is.

But unfortunately this idea flopped, because they failed to take into account two things.

One, the fact that criminals exist.
And two, the fact that coloured paint exists.

But the idea was fantastically optimistic and deserved to succeed.

A better version of this might be to ask people to recycle their books. Give them to a charity shop, your local library, or just leave them lying on a park bench.

Photo: Sara Morris

Happiness is a fairly traded banana

Fair-trade products guarantee to give the people who grow them a fair share of the profits. You'll see all sorts of fair-trade products in the shops these days – from bananas to coffee. So, if you buy a fair-trade banana, you can be proud of your banana.

And there are few feelings in this world that are better than being proud of your banana.

Nice to do. Nice to get. What is there not to like about it?

ever told you this, but…

re what we do ©

Royal Mail

Photo: John Lamb / Getty Images

Don't just do something.
Sit there.

Right now 12 million people in the UK
are on antidepressants.

Depression affects a huge number of people.
But there are lots of little things we can all
do to make the world a less depressing place.

Like... just listening.

It's a real art, actually – and not as easy as it sounds.

Listen to someone, don't make any comments,
don't try to solve their problems.

Just listen.

We're
OPEN

Come on in and have a look around. How are you today?
We've got some of those biscuits you said you liked.
They're turning out to be quite a popular choice down the street.
Oh, don't worry if you haven't got enough change on you, just
give it to me next time you're in.

See you tomorrow.

Illustration: Andy Hammond at illustrationweb.com

Photo: Nick Walker / Oliver Davies

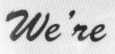

We're CLOSED

So sorry, hope you don't need anything too urgent.
The thing is, not enough of you have been coming to see us recently. We think it might have something to do with the big shop that's opened up down the road.
We've loved being here but just can't afford to stay open any more.

See you.

www.

camra.org.uk
british-naturism.org.uk
burmacampaign.org.uk
marssociety.org.uk
amnesty.org
howardleague.org
co-op.co.uk/membership
greenpeace.org
nationaltrust.org.uk
maketradefair.org
anthonynolan.org.uk/
neighbourhoodwatch.net
thewinesociety.com
ramblers.org.uk
labour.org.uk
conservatives.com
rspb.org.uk
farmgarden.org.uk
sherlock-holmes.org.uk
thearchers.co.uk
sealedknot.org.uk
womens-institute.co.uk
tuc.org.uk
girlguiding.org.uk/info/
scouts.org.uk
realrunner.com
embroiderersguild.com
local-history.co.uk/Groups
stonewall.org.uk/stonewall
harpsichord.org.uk
trombone-society.org.uk
sk8uk.co.uk
campingandcaravanningclub.co.uk
thebritishmuseum.ac.uk
museum.scotland.net
poetrysociety.org.uk
welsh-canoeing.org.uk
woodland-trust.org.uk
philiplarkin.com
debating.org
belfastzoo.co.uk/home.asp
snowdonia-society.org.uk
britsurf.org
britishlegion.org.uk
dinosaursociety.com
cartography.org.uk/index.html
ukphilately.org.uk/nps
fawcettsociety.org.uk
tonyhancock.org.uk
music-hall-society.com

Long gone are the days when joining something meant socks and sandals in the local church hall and a feisty jostle for the last Jammie Dodger at half time.

These days, joining in can simply mean logging on.

Photo: Branka Jukić

A friend of mine has
never forgotten seeing
his father kiss his
grandad's hand as
he lay in a coma,
just before he died.

It was the only time
he had ever seen
them kiss.

And the only time he
hugged his father was
when his sister died.

It wasn't that they
weren't close, just that
they were grown up,
they were men, and
British, and only death
could take down all
the barriers.

But children do it
instinctively – they want
to touch and be touched,
to hold and be held.

So if there was one bit
of advice we'd give
everyone reading this
book, it would be this.

Touch someone you love.

Hold them.

Stroke them.

Kiss them.

It's the one piece of
magic we can all do,
every day.

Illustration: Tim Ashton

Every year thousands of pairs of specs could be flown to developing countries

Many of us have old pairs of glasses lying around unused. Yet 200 million people around the world need glasses every year. People who can't see properly can't do their jobs, and kids who can't see properly can't learn at school.

So don't bin your old bins. Recycle 'em.

Contact www.vao.org.uk

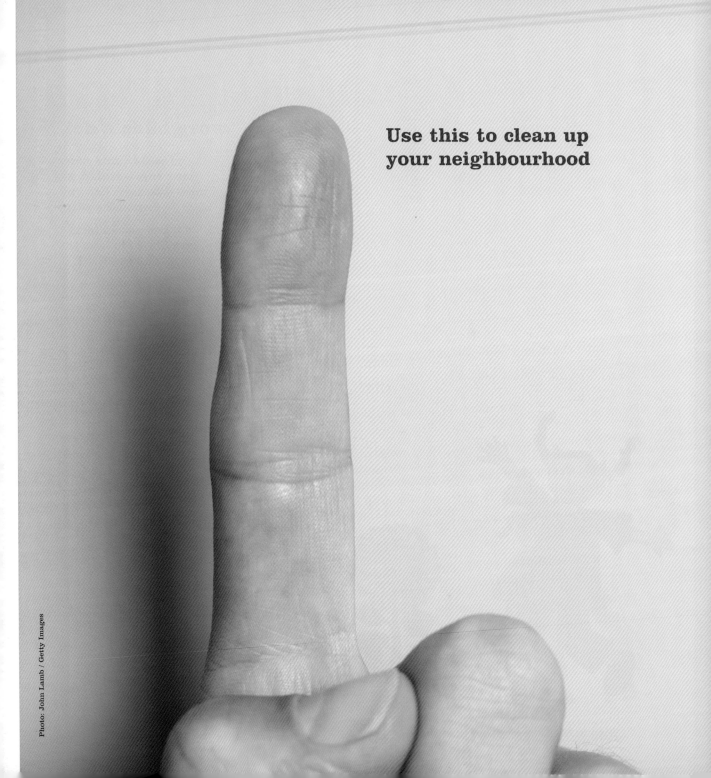

Use this to clean up
your neighbourhood

Photo: John Lamb / Getty Images

If you see some rubbish on the street in your area, it's very easy to just go 'tsk tsk' and do nothing about it.

And quite good fun too, because going 'tsk tsk' is strangely addictive.

But if you ring your local council, they're obliged to come and clean it up.

You can find the number on www.tagish.co.uk and store it in your mobile.

It's a win–win because the street looks nicer, and you get something back for your council tax.

Talk to strangers.
Start next door.

Give your phone number
to 5 people in your street.

Why not?

They could help you, you
could help them, you could
make new friends.

My name is: _____

I'm your neighbour

My phone number is: _____

Please call if I can help

My name is: _____

I'm your neighbour

My phone number is: _____

Please call if I can help

My name is: _____

I'm your neighbour

My phone number is: _____

Please call if I can help

My name is: _____

I'm your neighbour

My phone number is: _____

Please call if I can help

My name is: _____

I'm your neighbour

My phone number is: _____

Please call if I can help

we are what we do©

we are what we do©

we are what we do©

we are what we do©

we are what we do©

Use of every paper

Over 350 million trees are cut down every year
for the paper that's used in UK offices alone.

So much for the so-called paperless office which everyone
was writing all-staff memos about a few years back.

But if we used both sides of the sheet – for instance
by pressing the button that says 'use both sides of
the paper' on the photocopier – we could halve this.

Let's create a culture in which we make it socially
unacceptable to use only one side of paper.

both

sides

piece

of

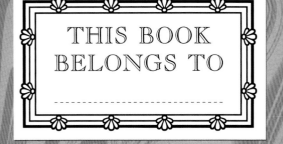

THIS BOOK
BELONGS TO

Isn't this a little bit self serving,
an advertisment for our book in
the middle of our book?

But this isn't about making
money it's about making change.

For change to really happen at
least a million people have to
adopt the actions in this book.

So, after you've bought your copy,
buy another.

And then give it to the person
you think needs it most.
You know the one.

Photo: Paul Schutzer / Time Life / Getty Images

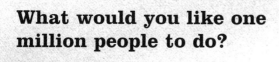

What would you like one million people to do?

One man or woman can change the way we act every day.
One such man was Martin Luther King.

Send us your ideas for what you'd like one
million people to do, and we'll make them part
of the We Are What We Do movement.

suggestions@wearewhatwedo.org

The simple actions in this book are just a beginning.
Discover more from these websites and go further. We are what we do.

01	DECLINE PLASTIC BAGS WHENEVER POSSIBLE	www.recoup.org/business/default.asp
02	READ A STORY WITH A CHILD	www.dfes.gov.uk/read
		www.readtogether.co.uk
03	FIT AT LEAST ONE ENERGY-SAVING LIGHT BULB	www.est.org.uk
04	LEARN BASIC FIRST AID	www.sja.org.uk
		www.redcross.org.uk/forstaid
05	SMILE AND SMILE BACK	www.lotsajokes.com
06	TAKE PUBLIC TRANSPORT WHEN YOU CAN	www.pti.org.uk
		www.liftshare.com
07	PLANT A TREE	www.woodland-trust.org.uk/index.htm
		www.rsatrees.org/plantatree
08	HAVE A BATH WITH SOMEONE YOU LOVE	www.british-naturism.org.uk
09	IF IT SAYS 30MPH, DO 30MPH	www.thinkroadsafety.gov.uk
10	TURN YOUR THERMOSTAT DOWN BY 1°	www.natenergy.org.uk/ensave1.htm
11	GET FITTER, FEEL BETTER	www.whi.org.uk
		www.walktoschool.org.uk
12	TURN OFF APPLIANCES AT THE MAINS	www.greenenergy.org.uk
13	RECYCLE YOUR MOBILE PHONE	www.fonebak.org
		www.oxfam.org.uk/what_you_can_do/recycle/phones.htm
14	SPEND TIME WITH SOMEONE FROM A DIFFERENT GENERATION	www.ageconcern.org.uk
		www.contact-the-elderly.org
15	REGISTER ONLINE AS AN ORGAN DONOR	www.uktransplant.org.uk/thesolution
16	GIVE YOUR CHANGE TO CHARITY	www.unicef.org/infobycountry/uk_change_for_good.html
17	TRY WATCHING LESS TV	www.healthunit.org/physact/home/tv_off/tvturn_off.htm
		www.whitedot.org
18	LEARN TO BE FRIENDLY IN ANOTHER LANGUAGE	www.cilt.org.uk
		www.bbc.co.uk/languages
19	LEARN ONE GOOD JOKE	www.ahajokes.com
		www.azkidsnet.com
20	FIND OUT HOW YOUR MONEY IS INVESTED	news.bbc.co.uk/1/hi/programmes/moneybox/default.stm
		www.eiris.org
21	TURN OFF UNNECESSARY LIGHTS	www.dark-skies.org.uk
		www.saveenergy.co.uk
22	USE YOUR WILL TO GOOD EFFECT	www.searchwill.co.uk
		www.which.net
		www.ethicalwill.com
23	HAVE MORE MEALS TOGETHER	www.parenthood.com/recipe.html
24	PUT YOUR GUM IN THE BIN	www.encams.org/home/home.asp
25	USE A MUG NOT A PLASTIC CUP	www.wasteonline.org.uk

26	GIVE BLOOD	www.blood.co.uk
		www.scotblood.co.uk
		www.nibts.org
		www.welsh-blood.org.uk
27	PAY MORE WHEN YOU BUY AT CHARITY SHOPS	www.charityshops.org.uk
28	SEIZE THE MOMENT	www.stanford.edu/group/king
		www.mkgandhi.org
29	RECYCLE YOUR COMPUTER	www.computer-aid.org
		www.tfs.org.uk
30	BAKE SOMETHING FOR A FRIEND	www.joyofbaking.com
31	TURN OFF THE TAP WHILST BRUSHING YOUR TEETH	www.environment-agency.gov.uk/subjects/waterres
32	DO SOMETHING YOU THINK YOU CAN'T DO	www.learndirect.co.uk
33	RECYCLE YOUR BOOKS	www.oxfam.org.uk
		www.bookcrossing.com
34	BUY FAIRLY TRADED PRODUCTS	www.fairtrade.org.uk
		www.maketradefair.com
35	WRITE TO SOMEONE WHO INSPIRED YOU	www.postoffice.co.uk
		www.bbc.co.uk/dna/getwriting
36	TAKE TIME TO LISTEN	www.readthesigns.org
		www.mind.org.uk
37	LET AT LEAST ONE CAR IN ON EVERY JOURNEY	www.theaa.com
		www.rac.co.uk
38	DON'T OVERFILL YOUR KETTLE	www.wateraid.org.uk
		www.ofwat.gov.uk
39	SHOP LOCALLY	www.regionalfoodanddrink.co.uk
		www.farmersmarkets.net
40	JOIN SOMETHING	www.wearewhatwedo.org
		www.join-me.co.uk
41	HUG SOMEONE	www.b-p-s-a.org.uk/hints_about_hugs.htm
42	RECYCLE YOUR SPECS	www.vao.org.uk
		www.ukorbis.org/bins/index.asp
43	GROW SOMETHING WITH A CHILD	www.bbc.co.uk/gardening/children
		www.wigglywigglers.co.uk
44	REPORT DUMPED RUBBISH TO YOUR COUNCIL	www.tagish.co.uk
45	GIVE YOUR PHONE NUMBER TO 5 PEOPLE IN YOUR STREET	www.upmystreet.com
46	USE BOTH SIDES OF EVERY PIECE OF PAPER	www.wasteconnect.co.uk
		www.paper.org.uk
47	BUY A COPY OF THIS BOOK FOR A FRIEND	www.wearewhatwedo.org
48	SEND US AN ACTION	www.wearewhatwedo.org
49	LEARN MORE, DO MORE	www.wearewhatwedo.org
50	DO SOMETHING FOR NOTHING	www.timebank.org.uk
		www.youthnet.org

We Are What We Do does not receive money from any websites mentioned in this book and is not responsible for their content. If you would like us to add your organisation to the list, please email us at suggestions@wearewhatwedo.org

Many people have contributed to
the creation of this book.

We would especially like to thank
the following:

Illustration Ltd for working with their
illustrators to create the images.
In particular, we would like to thank
Juliette Lott for coordination.

Getty Images for collaboration on
the photography. In particular, we
would like to thank Lewis Blackwell,
Zoë Whishaw and Emma Sutton.

The Book Service (part of the Random
House Group) for providing storage
and distribution, especially Mark Williams
and Nathalie Gelderman.

Innocence and **ArthurSteenAdamson**
for the creation of the We Are What
We Do brand.

Wieden + Kennedy for creative support
throughout the development of We Are
What We Do.

Nick Walker for production management
for We Are What We Do.

Cathay Pacific for providing travel facilities.

Alun Crockford
Andrew Selby
Andy Hammond
Andy Helme
Andy Holmes
Angus Fowler
Annabel Eatherley
Anne Shewring
Ashley Koo
Aurea Carpenter
Branka Jukić
Bryan Mullennix
Bryn Attewell
Camilla Harrisson
Caroline Mills
Carolyn Francis
Chalkie Davis
Chris O'Shea
Chris Walker
Chris Wigan
David Day
Ellie Robinson
Gail Greengross
Giles Gibbons
Gray Jolliffe
Graham Pugh

Hailey Phillips
John Lamb
Judy Lambert
Juliette Lott
Karen Baxter
Kate Poland
Ken Hoggins
Kevin Anthony Horgan
Lewis Blackwell
Mark George
Mark Robinson
Marksteen Adamson
Martin Crockatt
Michael Johnston
Mick Bailey
Mike Reid
Natalie Conn
Neil Christie
Nicholla Longley
Nick Walker
Niki Bowers
Nuala Donnelley
Oliver Davies
Olivia Rayner
Olivia Tebutt
Paul Daviz

Paul Schutzer
Paul Twivy
Peter Eatherley
Poppy Ashton
Rebecca Nicolson
Robert Ramsey
Russell Davies
Ruth Palmer
Sara Morris
Sara Smith-Laing
Sarah Walker
Shannon Fagan
Sholto Walker
Sophie Hayes
Spencer Jones
Stephen Chernin
Steve Henry
Steve Hilton
Struan Wallace
Stuart Holmes
Stuart Simmons
Sue Souchaud
Tim Ashton
Tony Davidson
Willie Ryan
Zoë Whishaw

Companies:
Antidote
Allen & Overy LLP
Apna Ghar
Brunswick Group
Business in the Community
Channel 4
Community Links
Good Business
Interbrand
Lyndales Solicitors
Royal Mail
Short Books
Three Blind Mice
TimeBank
Time Life
White Door

Thank you.

we are what we do ☺